21st Century Skills Library

D0005337

REAL WORLD MATH: NATURAL DISASTERS

DROUGHTS

BY VICKY FRANCHINO

Published in the United States of America by
Cherry Lake Publishing, Ann Arbor, Michigan
www.cherrylakepublishing.com

Content Adviser
Jack Williams
Founding editor of the *USA Today* weather page and author of *The AMS Weather Book: The Ultimate Guide to America's Weather*

Math Adviser
Katherine M. Gregory, M.Ed

Credits
Cover and page 1, ©Javier Etcheverry/Alamy; page 4, ©Happystock/Dreamstime.com; page 6, ©Vishwa Kiran/Dreamstime.com; page 8, ©Franz Pfluegl/Dreamstime.com; page 10, ©Sofiaworld/Dreamstime.com; page 12, ©Meduzzu/Dreamstime.com; page 14, ©Clearviewstock/Dreamstime.com; page 16, ©Komelau/Dreamstime.com; page 20, ©Egonzitter/Dreamstime.com; page 22, ©Robyn Mackenzie/Shutterstock, Inc. page 24, ©Swatchandsoda/Dreamstime.com; page 26, ©Perkmeup/Dreamstime.com; page 28, ©Paul Prescott/Shutterstock, Inc.

Library of Congress Cataloging-in-Publication Data
Franchino, Vicky.
  Droughts / by Vicky Franchino.
    p. cm.—(Real world math)
  Includes bibliographical references and index.
  ISBN 978-1-61080-322-9 (lib. bdg.)—ISBN 978-1-61080-331-1 (e-book)—ISBN 978-1-61080-407-3 (pbk.)
  1. Droughts—Juvenile literature. 2. Drought forecasting—Juvenile literature. 3. Mathematics—Juvenile literature. I. Title. II. Series.
  QC929.25.F74 2012
  551.57'73—dc23   2011030957

Cherry Lake Publishing would like to acknowledge
the work of The Partnership for 21st Century Skills.
Please visit *www.21stcenturyskills.org* for more information.

Printed in the United States of America
Corporate Graphics Inc.
January 2012
CLSP10

TABLE OF CONTENTS

CHAPTER ONE
WHAT IS A DROUGHT?

When most people hear the phrase "natural disasters," they think of hurricanes, forest fires, or earthquakes. These are catastrophes, and they happen very quickly. It's easy to see the destruction they cause.

But there's another type of natural disaster that's just as serious, even if it isn't as dramatic or as sudden. It's called a

Crops fail when they do not receive enough water.

drought. Droughts happen whenever an area gets less **precipitation** than usual for a long enough time to cause big problems. Droughts can occur in both dry places and wet places. Droughts are serious because they cause crops and animals to die and people to lose their jobs. In poor countries, droughts usually result in a food shortage.

 LIFE & CAREER SKILLS

The Palmer Drought Severity Index is a tool used to measure drought. Meteorologist Wayne Palmer developed the index in 1965. The index rates drought on a number system that runs from −4 to +4. The number *0* is used to show a normal amount of moisture. An area with a rating below *0* is drier than normal. If the rating is above *0*, the area is wetter than normal. Scientists determine the number by studying an area's precipitation amounts, its temperature, and how much moisture is in the soil.

There are many different types of drought. A meteorological drought means there is less precipitation than usual. A hydrological drought occurs when lakes and rivers have lower-than-normal water levels. Agricultural droughts happen when there isn't enough water to grow crops.

Sometimes areas are naturally very dry. This means that water always has to be brought to that area. The city of Las Vegas, Nevada, is an example. Some parts of the world have natural dry seasons. There is enough rain at certain times of the year and very little rain at others. Costa Rica and India are two countries with natural dry seasons.

There is even such a thing as an invisible drought. This means that high temperatures cause most rainwater to evaporate, or go back into the air, before it can soak into the ground.

India's dry season usually lasts from October to June.

REAL WORLD MATH CHALLENGE

The chart below shows the average monthly precipitation in two U.S. cities: Seattle, Washington, and Las Vegas, Nevada. Which city has the higher average annual precipitation? What is the difference in average annual precipitation between the two cities?

Average precipitation	Seattle, WA	Las Vegas, NV
January	5.4 in	0.5 in
February	4.0 in	0.5 in
March	3.5 in	0.4 in
April	2.3 in	0.3 in
May	1.7 in	0.3 in
June	1.5 in	0.1 in
July	0.8 in	0.4 in
August	1.1 in	0.5 in
September	1.9 in	0.3 in
October	3.3 in	0.3 in
November	5.8 in	0.4 in
December	5.9 in	0.4 in

(Turn to page 29 for the answers)

CHAPTER TWO

WHY DO DROUGHTS HAPPEN?

All the water that's in the world today has been here since Earth was first created. You're using the same water that was around at the time of the dinosaurs!

Snowstorms are part of Earth's water cycle.

The water we use today has gone through many changes. That's because water constantly moves through the **water cycle**. During this cycle, water exists in different forms and moves from one place to another.

Water that starts as a liquid in a river, lake, or ocean is heated by the Sun and turned into a gas called **water vapor**. This gas rises into the air and turns into droplets that form clouds. The clouds are carried from one place to another by air currents. Eventually, the water falls back to the earth in the form of rain, hail, snow, or sleet, and returns to bodies of water so the cycle can begin all over again.

The water cycle, however, doesn't always operate so smoothly. When it doesn't, an area can have a drought or, the opposite, a flood.

Changes in **air pressure** can affect the water cycle. Air pressure is the force with which the air presses against everything. This force is caused by gravity. Air rises when there is low air pressure at ground level. This rising air carries water vapor, which can create clouds and precipitation. Air sinks when there is high pressure at ground level. The high pressure prevents the air from rising to create clouds and precipitation. If a high-pressure system stays in an area for a long time, it can cause a drought.

The water cycle can also be affected by changes in the water. Two examples are the weather patterns called El Niño and La Niña. During El Niño, the water in the Pacific Ocean near the equator is unusually warm. This results in more rainfall on the west coast of North and South America, and less rainfall in Indonesia and Australia. During La Niña, the opposite happens. The waters in the Pacific are unusually cold, and there is more rainfall in Indonesia and Australia.

To help farmers grow food during a drought, scientists are experimenting with new kinds of corn and other crops.

LEARNING & INNOVATION SKILLS

Food shortages are one of the biggest problems caused by drought. To solve the problem, seed companies and scientists are working to create seeds that can grow in dry conditions. These seeds are created through genetic modification. This means that scientists have changed the genetic makeup of the plant in a laboratory. They mixed features from different plants to make a new "super" plant. For instance, a scientist might create a plant that needs less water, can grow at higher temperatures, and is more nutritious. Some people believe that genetically altered seeds might create food that is unsafe to eat. Others argue that the seeds are safe and that it is more important to make sure the world has enough food. What do you think?

Many scientists believe that human actions can affect droughts. One way is through global warming. Most cars and the equipment that creates electricity burn fossil fuels such as oil and coal for energy. These fuels release carbon dioxide into Earth's atmosphere. Carbon dioxide blocks heat from escaping Earth. This could be making Earth warmer than it once was. Warming Earth changes weather patterns, which can make drought worse in some places while bringing more rain to other places.

Humans also make droughts worse through deforestation, or cutting down trees. Trees, like all growing plants, help prevent soil from washing away. They also add moisture to the air through a process called **transpiration**.

Damaging deforestation has taken place in many places, including the Carpathian Mountains in Romania.

Sometimes an area can experience drought even when it receives the same amount of rain it normally would. This happens when an area's population increases, and the need for water increases along with it. As the world's population grows, so does the risk of drought.

REAL WORLD MATH CHALLENGE

Mountain snow is an important source of freshwater, especially in the western parts of the United States. Scientists use different methods to determine how much freshwater they will get from snowfall. One way is by measuring the snowpack, which is the snow that falls naturally on the ground. Let's say you had a flat field that was 500 feet long and 200 feet wide. If it was covered in 2 inches of snow, how many cubic feet of snowpack would there be? Hint: Think of the snow as if it's shaped like a box and that you are measuring the volume of the box.

(Turn to page 29 for the answers)

CHAPTER THREE

DO THE MATH: DROUGHTS AROUND THE WORLD

Droughts have occurred throughout Earth's history. We learn about past droughts in several ways. Often, droughts have been recorded in written histories that still

Drought can cause entire lakes to dry up and disappear.

exist. Scientists also study trees and soil to learn about droughts that happened hundreds of years ago. For example, the rings on a tree's trunk are wider in years with sufficient rainfall and thinner in years when there was a shortage of rain. Soil layers often contain information that tells scientists about the amount of water at different times in history.

Archaeologists have found evidence to show that Akkad, present-day Syria and Iraq, was probably destroyed by drought around 2200 BCE. At about the same time, a long-lasting drought likely wiped out the Egyptian Old Kingdom. Scientists have also found signs that ancient civilizations in Central and South America, such as the Maya, ended because of drought.

China has suffered from many terrible droughts. From 1876 to 1879 CE, a drought in eastern China is believed to have killed as many as 13 million people. China suffered another drought in the 1920s that likely killed about half a million people. Recent droughts may not have killed as many people as those in the past, but they still cause hardships for millions. China had a serious drought in 2001, and in 2011 the mighty Yangtze River was at the lowest level it had been in half a century.

In the last several decades, Australia has experienced numerous droughts. In 1982 and 1983, the combination of a drought and a heat wave caused a horrible fire. During the first decade of the 21st century, Australia suffered from a drought that was called the Big Dry. It was the worst drought in many years. Farmers were forced to sell their animals because they had no water for them. In many areas, wild camels and snakes came out of the wilderness and into populated areas, searching for water.

The Sahel region of northern Africa has experienced extreme levels of drought in the last 30 years. Millions of people have died from drought-related **starvation** and

People in Kenya stand in line to receive a share of rice.

illness. Millions of **refugees** have fled their drought-stricken countries and moved to other places. Many nations have tried to send water, food, and supplies to help the people of Africa. But this aid does not always get to the people who need it most.

The worst drought to hit the United States occurred between 1931 and 1938. It affected almost every state in the country. Bad farming practices made the water shortage even worse, especially in the Midwest.

 LIFE & CAREER SKILLS

As the drought of the 1930s continued, the U.S. government set up numerous departments and organizations to protect the soil and conserve water. In 1935, the Soil Conservation Service was established. Today, it is called the Natural Resources Conservation Service (NRCS). The NRCS works with farmers and other landowners to help them understand the best ways to use their land. It shows them techniques designed to protect and preserve soil, water, air, plants, and animals. The first chief of the organization, Hugh Hammond Bennett, said, "If we take care of the land, it will take care of us."

Before farmers settled in the area, the **prairies** were covered with tough grasses. These grasses did not require a lot of water to survive. Their strong roots held the soil in place. Throughout the 19th and early 20th centuries, midwestern farmers plowed up millions of acres of these grasses to plant crops. The crops they planted did not have the same strong roots as the grasses. During the drought of the 1930s, the rich soil turned into dust. Without strong roots to hold it, the dust blew everywhere. The prairie states soon had a new name: the Dust Bowl.

REAL WORLD MATH CHALLENGE

How much water do you use in a day? Look at the list below and determine how many times a day you do each activity. How many gallons of water do you use each day?

Activity	Number of gallons of water required
Flushing a toilet	3 gallons
Brushing your teeth	1 gallon
Washing your hands	1 gallon
Taking a shower	2.5 gallons per minute
Taking a bath	50 gallons

(Turn to page 29 for the answers)

Dust covered buildings and roads. Plows typically used for removing snow were used to plow dust. Cattle and sheep choked to death on dust. Families lived in dust-covered houses. They stuck paper and cloth into every door and window crack to keep out the dust. Sometimes planes were unable to fly because their pilots could not see through the dust that filled the skies.

The United States also experienced a bad drought from 1987 to 1989. More than half of the country had less precipitation than usual. Dry trees and arid land made wildfires a terrible danger. About 800,000 acres (324,000 hectares) in Yellowstone National Park were destroyed or damaged by out-of-control fires.

In 2011, many parts of the United States experienced another lengthy drought. Most of the southern states had seen little rain in many, many months. The drought damaged crops and forced farmers to reduce their livestock herds. It also contributed to dangerous fires.

CHAPTER FOUR
DO THE MATH: HOW DOES DROUGHT AFFECT US?

Droughts can cause many different types of problems. Some problems are merely inconveniences. For instance, if your city had a drought, you might not be able

Many farmers use sprinklers to make sure their crops receive enough water.

to water your lawn as often as usual. You might have to take shorter showers or do fewer loads of laundry.

Most problems caused by drought, however, are very serious and even life threatening. One of the most serious problems is damage to crops. When there isn't enough rain, farmers either have to **irrigate** their crops or watch them dry up and die. But irrigation is expensive, and many farmers cannot afford it. If a crop fails, people who rely on that food for a large part of their diet may go hungry. During the 1980s, millions of people in Africa died because drought destroyed crops.

LEARNING & INNOVATION SKILLS

Humans have no control over when it rains or snows. Or do they? Some people believe that a technique called cloud seeding can produce precipitation. A material called silver iodide has a structure that is very similar to that of ice. Some scientists believe that by shooting pieces of silver iodide into the clouds, rain or snow can be created. Cloud seeding has been practiced for many years, but it is hard to tell how effective it is. That's because it can never be known whether a cloud that rains after seeding might have rained anyway.

Drought can also force people to leave their homes. In many African countries, people have fled their homeland because they faced starvation. Many had nowhere to go. Camps were set up for these refugees. But people are often exposed to life-threatening diseases in such crowded camps. Can you imagine having to leave your country because there wasn't enough food?

Droughts can also lead to fires. When rainfall is scarce, brush, trees, and other plants become very dry and can burn quickly. In 2009, long-term drought was a factor in a huge bushfire in Australia that killed more than 200 people. In 2010, fires destroyed much of the wheat crop in drought-

Bushfires can destroy houses, cars, and the surrounding wildlife.

REAL WORLD MATH CHALLENGE

Each year, the United States loses billions of dollars because of droughts, floods, and hurricanes. Use the numbers in the chart below to answer these questions. What is the total amount of money that the United States loses each year because of these types of natural disasters? How much more money does the United States lose on droughts compared to hurricanes? [Hint: Both of your answers will be ranges because some of the averages are shown as ranges.]

	Droughts	Floods	Hurricanes
Annual average	$6 billion–$8 billion	$2.4 billion	$1.2 billion–$4.8 billion

(Turn to page 29 for the answers)

stricken areas of Russia. Drought and fires are becoming more common in South America's Amazon rain forest. Loggers cut down too many trees there. This removes the forest's natural protection.

Droughts destroy habitats for animals and can destroy human habitats, too. In many areas, large underground **reservoirs** have been built to hold water. If there is a drought, the land above the reservoir may crack, and buildings can sink or fall into these huge underground holes.

CHAPTER FIVE
PROTECTING THE EARTH'S WATER SUPPLY

I n 2011, there were 7 billion people on Earth. Experts predict that by the year 2050, there will probably be more

Many scientists believe that fossil fuels contribute to changes in the weather. Renewable energy from wind farms helps to cut the use of fossil fuels.

than 9 billion. Each one of these people will need water, so it's important to find effective ways to manage Earth's water supply.

Many scientists believe that climate change causes droughts to happen more frequently and to be more extreme. They believe that if people reduced their use of fossil fuels, the effects of climate change might be lessened. Renewable energy, such as solar, water, and wind, can replace fossil fuels.

21ST CENTURY CONTENT

Oceans cover about 70 percent of Earth's surface. So it might seem like there's plenty of water to meet the world's growing needs. Almost all of Earth's water, however, is saltwater, which cannot be used for drinking or growing food. Saltwater can be made usable through **desalination**. In this process, salt is removed from water to make it suitable for drinking or irrigation. Scientists are currently working on methods to reduce the high cost of desalination. If they are successful, freshwater can be made available to people living in regions where water is limited or becoming limited. Most of the world's desalinated water is used in the desert countries of the Middle East.

Another way to protect Earth's water supply is by using less of it. At home, you can take shorter showers and turn off the water as you brush your teeth. Your parents can replace appliances with ones that use less water. In your yard, you can choose plants that require less water to thrive. Some people find ways to reuse their "gray" water. That is the water used for activities such as laundry and doing the dishes.

You can save as much as eight gallons a day by turning off the water while you brush your teeth.

Farmers can save water by changing how they grow crops. One method is conservation tillage, in which farmers leave the plant materials from past harvests on the soil's surface. This helps conserve the moisture in the soil and prevents soil erosion. A brand-new technology that uses sensors on orbiting satellites is currently being tested. If successful, the technology will be able to tell farmers exactly how much water to use when irrigating their crops. That way, there is no waste of the precious resource.

If we all do our part, we can help make sure everyone has the water they need.

REAL WORLD MATH CHALLENGE

According to the U.S. National Center for Atmospheric Research, droughts are happening more frequently than ever. In the 30-year period between the 1970s and the early 2000s, the amount of the world that was suffering from serious droughts doubled. Today, about 30 percent of the world is affected by severe drought. If the rate of drought continues to double, how much of the world will have to deal with dangerous water shortages in 30 years? How much in 60 years?

(Turn to page 29 for the answers)

Usable water can be hard to come by, even in cities.

REAL WORLD MATH CHALLENGE ANSWERS

Chapter One

Page 7

Seattle, WA, has the higher annual precipitation.

Seattle: 5.4 + 4.0 + 3.5 + 2.3 + 1.7 + 1.5 + 0.8 + 1.1 + 1.9 + 3.3 + 5.8 + 5.9 = 37.2 total inches

Las Vegas: 0.5 + 0.5 + 0.4 + 0.3 + 0.3 + 0.1 + 0.4 + 0.5 + 0.3 + 0.3 + 0.4 + 0.4 = 4.4 total inches

The difference between the two cities is 32.8 inches.

37.2 − 4.4 = 32.8 inches

Chapter Two

Page 13

The total volume is 2,400,000 cubic feet.

500 feet × 12 inches per foot = 6,000 inches long

200 feet × 12 inches per foot = 2,400 inches wide

6,000 inches × 2,400 inches × 2 inches = 28,800,000 cubic inches of snow

28,880,000 cubic inches ÷ 12 inches per foot = 2,400,000 cubic feet

Chapter Three

Page 18

Each person uses different amounts of water each day.

Multiply the number of times you perform each activity by the amount of water the activity uses.

Add these numbers together to find the total amount of water you use each day.

Chapter Four

Page 23

The United States loses $9.6 billion to $15.2 billion each year.

6 + 2.4 + 1.2 = $9.6 billion

8 + 2.4 + 4.8 = $15.2 billion

The country spends $3.2 billion to $4.8 billion more on droughts than on hurricanes.

6 − 1.2 = $4.8 billion

8 − 4.8 = $3.2 billion

Chapter Five

Page 27

If the amount of the world suffering from drought doubled in 30 years, 60% of the world will suffer from drought.

30% × 2 = 60%

If the number doubled again in another 30 years, 100% of the world would have a drought.

60% × 2 = 120%

It is not possible to cover more than 100% of the world.

GLOSSARY

air pressure (AIR PRESH-ur) the force with which the air presses against everything

desalination (dee-sa-luh-NAY-shuhn) removing salt from seawater

irrigate (IHR-uh-gate) to supply water to crops by artificial means, such as channels and pipes

prairies (PRAIR-eez) large areas of rolling grassland with few or no trees

precipitation (pri-sip-i-TAY-shuhn) rain, snow, hail, or sleet

refugees (ref-yuh-JEEZ) people forced to leave their homes because of natural disaster, war, or persecution

reservoirs (REZ-ur-vworz) large areas where water is collected and stored

starvation (star-VAY-shuhn) suffering or dying from lack of food

transpiration (transs-puh-RAY-shuhn) the process by which plants give off moisture into the atmosphere

water cycle (WAW-tur SYE-kuhl) the constant movement of the earth's waters

water vapor (WAW-tur VAY-pur) the gas produced when water evaporates

FOR MORE INFORMATION

BOOKS

Fradin, Judy, and Dennis Fradin. *Droughts*. Washington, DC: National Geographic, 2008.

Levey, Richard H. *Dust Bowl! The 1930s Black Blizzards.*
New York: Bearport Publishing Company, Inc., 2005.

Droughts. Chicago: World Book, 2009.

WEB SITES

National Drought Mitigation Center—Drought for Kids
http://drought.unl.edu/DroughtforKids.aspx
This Web site has lots of helpful information about what drought is, how scientists track it, and how we can reduce the risk of drought.

U.S. Drought Monitor
www.drought.unl.edu/dm/monitor.html
Is the part of the United States where you live experiencing a drought? Check out this site to learn the latest drought conditions and forecasts throughout America.

21ST CENTURY SKILLS LIBRARY

INDEX

ABOUT THE AUTHOR

Vicky Franchino has written dozens of nonfiction books for children and always enjoys learning about new subjects. She remembers the "We Are the World" concerts in 1985, which raised money for people dying of starvation because of droughts in Africa. Vicky lives with her husband and children in Madison, Wisconsin.